PREVENIENT GRACE

A (4-WEEK) STUDY

DAN BOONE

f·

THE FOUNDRY
PUBLISHING·

978-0-8341-4191-9

Printed in the
United States of America

Cover design: Rob Monacelli
Interior design: Sharon Page

Library of Congress Cataloging-in-Publication Data
A complete catalog record for this book is available from the Library of
Congress.

All Scripture quotations, unless indicated, are taken from the New Revised
Standard Version, Updated Edition (NRSVUE). Copyright © 2021 National
Council of Churches of Christ in the United States of America. Used by per-
mission. All rights reserved worldwide.

Scriptures marked (MSG) are taken from *The Message* (MSG). Copyright ©
1993, 2002, 2018 by Eugene H. Peterson. Used by permission of NavPress.
All rights reserved. Represented by Tyndale House Publishers, Inc.

The internet addresses, email addresses, and phone numbers in this book
are accurate at the time of publication. They are provided as a resource. The
Foundry Publishing does not endorse them or vouch for their content or
permanence.

10 9 8 7 6 5 4 3 2 1

CONTENTS

WEEK 1

Where Is God?

4

WEEK 2

Cornelius and Peter

20

WEEK 3

The God Who Tells Us Who We Are

36

WEEK 4

I Likes to Be Chose

52

WHERE IS GOD?

I am fascinated by the last book of our Holy Scripture, the Revelation of Jesus to John. In a world that is awash with superhero imagery, who wouldn't be intrigued by bright red horses, beasts out of the bottomless pit, and grass-hopper armies? For those who think the story of God is bland, read Revelation! I also love that it is filled with more titles for God than any other book. It seems like the writer ran a rake over the other sixty-five books of the Bible and collected all the titles. My favorite appears near the beginning: "'I am the Alpha and the Omega,' says the Lord God, who is and who was and who is to come, the Almighty" (1:8).

This title locates God in time. This is the Revelation of the God who is the beginning, the first, the Alpha, the A of our story—and also the God who is the end, the last, the Omega, the Z of our story. Our life is sandwiched between the presence of this God. The A-to-Z letters that spell out the story of our existence are all within the alphabet of God. From first to last breath and beyond, our life is lived in the presence of God.

There has not been a moment when God was not engaged with us. This was good news to people suffering in the wake of the Roman Empire and its beastly rule. The story of the Revelation placed them squarely inside the story and activity of God. They were not forgotten players on the world stage but people who mattered to the Almighty. They were living in the presence of the God *who is* with them in their present crisis, *who was* with them and with every human across time, and *who will be* with them in the next moment of consciousness.

We speak of prevenient grace as God seeking or finding us rather than us seeking or finding God because God has always been here. God is our past, present, and future. God is before us, with us, and in front of us. It's why the Revelation speaks of God as the beginning and the end, the first and the last, the Alpha and the Omega (the first and last letters of the Greek alphabet).

So how do you encounter God? By studying ancient scriptures to find divine fingerprints in human history? By watching the news to detect the activity of God in the present events? By peering into the morning sky and wondering what the future may bring? Yes, God is there. Past. Present. Future. God is there whether we know it or acknowledge it or experience it. Prevenient grace is the gift of God that opens us to experience God in our past, present, and future. God has gone ahead of our knowing, seeking, and experiencing to make us capable of receiving revelation.

As I think about the people to whom Revelation was written, I think they needed a reminder that the God who had been with them in the past, and was also with them in the present, was coming to them from their future. We know God because the God who has always known us stands in our future, enabling us to experience him. This is the gracious gift of prevenient grace—the grace that goes ahead of us and the grace that comes to us from the future.

God has gone ahead of
our knowing, seeking,
and experiencing to make
us capable of receiving
revelation.

Imagine if a young parent were teaching their crawling baby to walk for the first time. They get behind the infant, place their hands on the diaper, and aim the child into a room that is filled with wires to trip over, table edges to bump into, and obstacles to obstruct their path. Then they command the child to walk and give a gentle shove from the rear. They expect the child to do what the child has previously been unable to do. We'd give that parent an F, wouldn't we?

Imagine a different parent, who has been watching their child's development closely as the child grows, and knows when they are showing signs that they're ready to take their first steps. This parent clears the pathway ahead of time, positions the child next to something sturdy they can hold onto, crosses the room in front of the child, kneels at eye level with this infant they know intimately, opens their arms, and invites the child to come toward them. In that moment something occurs in the body of a baby. Suddenly they realize they can do what they were incapable of doing a moment before as they lean into and trust the love of the one who knows them. They walk into the future, not because someone shoved them from the rear and demanded it but because someone who knew them went before to prepare their path and then stood patiently waiting in the next moment, encouraging and inviting them forward.

It is hard to walk into our future when we are looking backward, but for some reason, we seem to think we can explain people into an experience with God simply by pointing to the past and telling them what God has done before. While that may give them some confidence, like a sturdy piece of furniture a child might lean on, it does not open them to the possibility that God has come in this present moment from their future to invite them to walk into life. Prevenient grace is about awakening to the God who stands in our future.

I wish I had understood this truth earlier in life. I've always read the Bible as a story of the *past* activity of God, and I've looked backward in time trying to locate God. But in truth, the Bible is the story of a God who shows up in the future.

In Genesis, God seems to run past the chaotic darkness that hovers over the deep and stands in front of it, from the future, calling creation into existence (see Genesis 1).

God gets ahead of Abram and tells him about blessings upon all people through the tribe that will come from his genes (Genesis 12).

God shows up in Midian before Moses arrives with his flock and burns from within a bush to deliver a people who are crying out in Egypt. These people don't even know that God has gone ahead to call Moses (Exodus 3).

God goes ahead of Mary and sends an angel to explain the upcoming pregnancy. God gets in front of Joseph's reasonable questions about this very pregnancy (Matthew 1; Luke 1).

God is always coming
to us from the future,
inviting us into his kingdom
that is coming.

God stands in the apostles' future, calling them to fish for a different kind of catch (Matthew 4:18–22; Luke 5:1–11).

God stands at Lazarus's tomb creating the next breath inside a corpse (John 11).

God goes ahead of Saul on the road to Damascus (Acts 9).

These stories from the past should give us confidence that God is standing in our future, creating it even as we live. And we are made capable of experiencing this God and participating in the future that only God can create for us. Prevenient grace does not expire when we experience the saving grace of God. God is always going before us— or, better yet, God is always coming to us from the future, inviting us into his kingdom that is coming.

When we pray, "Thy kingdom come," we are partic- ipating in a reality that is past, present, and future. This kingdom is assured by the resurrection of Jesus. Revela- tion proclaims him Lord of lords and King of kings (17:14). The grace of this kingdom is breaking into the present every time we are opened by God to experience its pow- er and presence. We are stepping into the future that has come to us in Christ.

If this reality is so transformative, why do many peo- ple know nothing about it? I often liken it to wireless or radio signals. It is possible that something is present, even at this very moment, of which we are totally unaware. Although we are made capable of experiencing God in this present moment, we are also given the freedom to resist this awareness. Resisting grace is a human freedom that God does not override. The more we practice this freedom, the easier it is to harden ourselves to the God who is present. I have often suggested to friends who do not know God to act as if God were present for one day: Talk to God. Listen for God. Look for God. See if there is any probing from God in the honest questions of their heart. Be open to a voice that speaks words of loving invitation. Be ready for unexpected gifts. I don't say this because I believe there is a formula of human searching that can always reliably find God. I say it because Scripture and experience both assure me that God is already there.

Sometimes this way of thinking about God standing in our future causes us to believe that God has already dictated the details of our lives. This perception turns God into a divine type of meteorologist or fortuneteller, whose forecasts or predictions—were God to make any—would definitely come true in the days ahead. If God operated that way, it would leave little room for us to fulfill our role as creative partners of God in the making of a life and a world. If it is all predetermined and laid out, God would only show up to tell us the forecast. The Christian life is much more creative than that. God invites humanity—starting with Adam and Eve but including us today—into a creative partnership where we tend creation and rule over it, together with the Creator. The future unfolds in our response to God. Sometimes it is a response of obedience, and the kingdom comes and God's will is done on earth even as it is done in heaven. Sometimes it is a response of disobedience, which leads to harmful consequences for humanity.

God's desired future for us is that we would be restored in the image and likeness of Jesus. This is the will of God for every creature. And God will stand in every future moment, as long as we have breath in our bodies, inviting us into this reality. Our lives are not pre-plotted. They unfold day by day based on how we do or do not respond to the grace God offers us. If I want to travel from New York to Los Angeles, there are many paths I can take. If I am free to do as I please on any given day, I may find myself moving toward or away from the desired destination. Prevenient grace indicates that God has a destination in mind for us: restoration in the image of Jesus. God will stand at every fork in the road, at every dead-end alley, and at every crossroad inviting us to choose the way that leads to life—but the choice remains our own to make.

God is already out in front of today. What will your next choice be?

JOURNALING AND REFLECTION

Pause to reflect on what you have read. What did you hear? Restate it in your own words. Make it your own. What is God pointing out in this chapter for you to think more about? What is God saying to you?

_____

_____

_____

_____

_____

_____

_____

_____

_____

_____

_____

_____

_____

_____

PRAYER

Imagine Jesus standing at the foot of your bed as you wake up, calling you into the day ahead. He is at work making all things new. What might Jesus say to you about the day ahead and about how you can join him in his work?

DISCUSSION

1. Define prevenient grace in your own words.

2. Where do you tend to look for God: your past, your present, or your future?

3. Share the story of how you first became aware of God and how you responded.

4. How do you view your future? As already determined and prearranged, or more like a choose-your-own-adventure novel that is being written daily?

5. What would you say to a friend who has never experienced God but indicates openness to the idea?

NOTES

NOTES

CORNELIUS AND PETER

If Revelation is interesting because of the imagery and symbolism, the book of Acts is interesting because of the wild ride the early followers of Jesus experience. The best way to describe the book is that some followers of Jesus who experienced the crucifixion and resurrection got on a ride called Pentecostal Power and hung on for dear life for twenty-eight chapters. The twists, turns, plunges, and surprises are as unpredictable as any journey ever imagined. God got out in front of his people, empowered them to be his witnesses, and then prepared the way ahead for their ministry.

I'm amazed at the action of the Spirit of the resurrected Jesus in Acts. Little did they know that tongues of fire and a mighty rushing wind were waiting for them in an upper room. Little did they know that they would testify to the Pentecostal experience in languages they'd never previously spoken so that everyone who had come from various nations and faraway places would understand them. Little did Peter and John know that their trip to the temple would result in a lame man walking, their being arrested, and a house-shaking prayer meeting. All through the book of Acts we can repeat, *little did they know*. But what we know now is that God was going ahead of them, directing their words and actions and opening the hearts of those who would hear the story of Jesus. The book of Acts is a grand story of the prevenient grace of God at work in the conversion of pagans and in the spread of the gospel.

Long before the Christian
mission gets to Cornelius in
Acts, God was already
on the scene.

One of my favorite stories in Acts is about Cornelius, whom we meet in chapter 10. He is a Roman centurion who lives in Caesarea. As a soldier of the empire, he is a pagan intruder in the eyes of God's people in Caesarea. But as we are introduced to him, we are told he is a devout man who fears God, gives generously to others, and prays often (v. 2). How does he know to do this? Has someone already introduced him to Jesus? Is he like the people David Busic writes about in *Way, Truth, Life*—the ones who dreamed about Jesus in regions where Christian evangelism was unlawful, or the tribes who saw the *Jesus Film* and declared that this man had already visited them?[1] Long before the Christian mission gets to Cornelius in Acts, God was already on the scene.

One day as Cornelius prays, God comes to him through an angel and tells him to summon a man from Joppa named Simon Peter. The angel even gives him the address where Peter is staying. So Cornelius sends his servants to fetch Peter (vv. 3–8). As they are on their way to retrieve Peter, God goes ahead of Peter to prepare him for the visit with Cornelius. Peter is not yet ready for the encounter.

Peter has gone up on the rooftop of the house in Joppa where he is staying to pray, and God is waiting for him there. When Peter's stomach suggests that it is

---

1. David A. Busic, *Way, Truth, Life: Discipleship as a Journey of Grace* (Kansas City, MO: The Foundry Publishing, 2021), 46–47.

time to eat, God offers him a vision: that of a sheet being lowered toward him, full of four-footed animals, reptiles, and birds—all of which have previously been declared by God to be unclean and unlawful for devout Jewish people to eat. In the vision, a voice tells Peter to get up, kill the creatures, and eat them. Being the holy man he is, Peter refuses because he knows God's law, and he is not willing to break it. The voice suggests that Peter should consider one thing: if God is putting it on the table, maybe it is not Peter's place to categorize it as unclean. The interaction happens three times (vv. 9–16). God's grace is persistent.

As Peter stands scratching his head on the roof, trying to make sense of what just happened, Cornelius's men appear at the front gate at that exact moment and ask for him. The Spirit tells Peter to listen to them and go with them because they are sent *by* the Spirit. Peter obeys, the men tell him about Cornelius, and Peter invites them to lodge with him for the night (vv. 17–23). Apparently, Peter is breaking Jewish purity protocol by hosting these gentiles and by agreeing to be hosted in Caesarea by Cornelius, another gentile.

The next day, they begin the two-day trip to Caesarea. By the time they arrive, Peter has apparently had enough time to reflect on his vision from Joppa and come to an understanding of what it means because he immediately declares his conclusion to Cornelius and everyone else who is listening: "You yourselves know that it is improper for a Jew to associate with or to visit an outsid-

God's grace is persistent.

er, but God has shown me that I should not call anyone profane or unclean. So when I was sent for, I came without objection. Now may I ask why you sent for me?" (vv. 28–29).

Cornelius repeats the story of his visit from the angel of God and invites Peter to tell him and his guests whatever God wishes, and that is how Peter ends up being the first Jewish Christian to preach the gospel of Christ to gentiles (vv. 30–43). As he speaks, the Holy Spirit falls upon the gathered crowd, and Peter is shocked that the Spirit is able to come to gentiles too, even as it came to him and his fellow Jewish believers back in Acts 2. They are all baptized in the name of Jesus (vv. 44–48).

God was doing a new thing once again, and even before God invited Peter to be part of it, God went ahead of Peter to pave the way for Peter's understanding and obedience. This is prevenient grace. Salvation does not come to Cornelius's home because humans had a planning conference on how to reach gentile military families. They did not draw up an evangelism strategy, raise funds, print slick salvation brochures, or go door-knocking in Caesarea. Salvation came in Caesarea because God moved, and the Spirit nudged.

This story reveals the prevenient grace that was at work in a man with little knowledge of Jesus and also in a man who had followed Jesus from the beginning of his public ministry. God came to Cornelius, but God also came to Peter to prepare him for the encounter. While

Salvation came in Caesarea
because God moved,
and the Spirit nudged.

many refer to this story as Cornelius's Conversion, it could also be called The Conversion of Peter's Categories. The penetrating grace of God shattered Peter's foundational and perfectly reasonable belief about the impurity of anything that was outside of Jewish tradition. It is true that Judaism was constructed as an exclusive religion to begin with, but it is also true that God always planned to expand it and make it inclusive for all. From the very first time that God called Abraham, God told him that God would build this nation of God's people *for the purpose* of eventually blessing (which involves including) *everyone* (Genesis 12:2–3). In Acts 10, God enacts this purpose more fully, starting with helping Peter to see everyone as God's creation, capable of being the same vessels of the Holy Spirit that the Jewish people were on the day of Pentecost in Acts 2.

When our walk with God becomes a collection of religious opinions and judgments about others, we become hardened into patterns that hinder us from moving in step with the activity of God in the world. This is why grace is needed in every form. The sanctifying work of God shatters and purifies our categories, enabling us to recognize the prevenient grace of God that is moving into the world as saving grace. We live from grace to grace.

The shattering of our categories requires that we be open to the experiences that God drops into our lap when we get quiet enough to pray. The wild ride of Pentecostal Power moves on the track that God lays before us even when we cannot see it or do not yet comprehend it. This is why the Christian life is called "the way." It is a track, a path, a road, a journey, an adventure with and toward God. Prevenient grace invites us to take the trip, but prevenient grace also prepares us and others for what God is doing.

Want to have some fun? Put your prevenient-grace glasses on. Read the book of Acts through that special lens and look for all the ways God is out in front of the apostles, opening people for the message about Jesus. Note the things that the apostles make happen versus the things that only God can make happen. Also note their awe as they experience being the hands and feet of Jesus in their world. That's a ride worth taking.

JOURNALING AND REFLECTION

Pause to reflect on what you have read. What did you hear? Restate it in your own words. Make it your own. What is God pointing out in this chapter for you to think more about? What is God saying to you?

_____

_____

_____

_____

_____

_____

_____

_____

_____

_____

_____

_____

_____

_____

PRAYER

Think about the people in your life whom God is actively seeking. Is there a picnic-blanket experience, like Peter's vision, that requires the sanctification of your categories to enable your participation in God's grace being extended to them? Keep in mind that God's grace is offered to others regardless of whether we participate. When we miss, ignore, or deny what God is doing in the lives of others, we are only short-changing ourselves.

DISCUSSION

1. When have you had a Cornelius moment in your life?

2. When have you had a Peter moment in your life, where God shattered your categories?

3. It has been said that much of what the church is attempting to do today can be done without the power of the Holy Spirit. What do you think about this statement? Is work that can be done without the Holy Spirit worthwhile work? What work might you do that would require God to work ahead of you?

4. Does your faith journey look more like a concrete set of beliefs that make things make sense, or is it more like a wild and unpredictable ride where anything might happen?

5. What do you suspect God is up to in your city these days? How might you participate?

NOTES

NOTES

THE GOD WHO TELLS US WHO WE ARE

I've spent more than forty years of my life on a college campus. College students represent a unique and usually transient portion of our population who are often testing the waters of independence and what it means to be human and to exist in community. It is not uncommon for college students to experience anxiety, depression, uncertainty, anger, and loneliness as they carry the weight of their childhoods and possibly past traumas while they press up against the hard edges of "the real world," many for the first time. College students and young adults of all generations have wrestled with their relationship to substances, media and technology, and social causes. And all this happens in a world that is and has always been bitterly divided on issues of sex, race, religion, and politics.

For some, this world is a thief that comes to steal joy, kill futures, and destroy meaningful life. We all live in this world and experience its formative influences. College students and young adults are not the first or the only ones to grapple with their own humanity and the meaning of existence, but they are perhaps uniquely positioned to consider these things more acutely. College specifically, and young adulthood more generally, is an obvious place and time to confront the reality that there is a way that leads to life and a way that leads to death and that the way we walk defines who we are.

Who am I? How will I live? What do I want? These may be the most important questions any of us will ever answer for ourselves. I am grateful for the writing of Alan

Noble in *You Are Not Your Own*, a book about identity, the behaviors that flow out of identity, and the meaning that is derived from these behaviors. At the core of many individuals' unsettled anxiety is a particular understanding of what it means to be human. That understanding is that we are our own selves and that we belong to and are accountable to—and only to—ourselves. If we believe this, and many of us do, then we might also believe that we must craft and create our own unique identity, that we must be our own moral compass, that we set our own boundaries for right and wrong, that nobody else has the right to be an authority over us, that our value lies in the world's recognition and affirmation of our self-created identity, and that we alone are responsible for building a meaningful life for ourselves.

Let's think about the natural consequences of the belief that we belong to ourselves. Certainly God gives us the freedom to do as we wish, but without God to identify us, affirm us, guide us, and define meaning for us, we are required to do all of that for ourselves because these things are necessary to being human. We will spend the rest of our lives creating and recreating our identity, demanding that the world affirm who we say we are, and looking for validation *from* the world—and all of that while everyone else around us is doing the same and coming up with the same empty, unsatisfying results.

Noble suggests that there are two pathways to take when we believe we are our own selves. The first path-

There is a way that leads to life and a way that leads to death, and the way we walk defines who we are.

way is *affirming.* I will rise to the challenge to be my best self, the true and authentic version of me. I will commit to self-improvement, optimize myself to be more and bigger and better. I will discipline myself to be the best. I will make something of myself. The world is perfectly wired to support my quest for my best self: how-to books, self-improvement gurus, performance gadgets. I can compete with my own performance because the world measures everything for me—how many steps I took today, how many hours of Netflix I watched, how fruitfully I slept, my body chemistry numbers, my GPA, my social media influence, my friends, my credit score, my weight, my unread messages, my bank balance. The world is perfectly shaped to help me improve by reminding me of the number I need to beat today in order to be better than I was yesterday. When I believe that I belong to myself, I am responsible for making myself valuable, so I will demand that the world recognize my value so that I feel special, loved, and as if I belong. Unfortunately, all of my achievements will never be enough to satisfy the longing inside me for affirmation.

The second pathway is *resigned.* Maybe I already tried the affirming pathway but learned I can never do enough or be enough to get the world to applaud my life. Perhaps I figured out that the world will not tell me I am unique, loved, and valued. Maybe the constant grind of competition is unappealing to me, so I may as well take my ball and go home because that is a more efficient use of my time. The world is perfectly wired to support my resignation. It will provide all the distractions I need to numb the ache in my soul. I can binge-watch myself into oblivion, eat, work, play video games, scroll social media, post endlessly, argue online, and blast the whole world with my opinions. The world is wired to put any distracting venture at my fingertips to keep me consuming until the day I die. I need never create my own identity again. I need only to consume whatever I desire because I am my own, and I belong to myself.

So how is prevenient grace good news for those of us who find ourselves on these pathways? I'm glad you asked! The fundamental lie of this world is that we are our own, that we belong only to ourselves. Until we see this lie for what it is, it will define us, rule us, and destroy us. We will eventually grow weary of being our own selves because humans were not created to make our own meaning, chart our own morality, or create our own identity. It certainly feels liberating, exhilarating, and even American to say things like "I am my own," "I chart my own path," or, "I make my own rules," but this way of life will leave us ragged, weary, aimless, and empty.

There is a word in the Christian vocabulary that defines this lie. The word is "sin." The essence of sin is self-sovereignty—the belief that we are our own. It's what Adam and Eve were after in the garden when they said no thanks to God and ate the forbidden fruit that would make them their own gods. God let them have their way, and the world as we know it has followed in their footsteps.

―――

Identity in Christ recognizes we are not our own.

―――

The good news for us is that there is a radically different understanding of what it means to be human. We are not our own—we belong to Christ. Our identity is found in Christ. Our ways, actions, and behaviors are guided by Christ. Our meaning is rooted in Christ. God tells us who we are, that we are valued as one created in God's image and likeness, that we belong to a people, that we are so loved that God would send his only Son to die on our behalf in order that we might be set free from the lie of the world. This God affirms our identity and guides us into the true expression of authentic humanity as God's created ones.

Yes, identity in Christ recognizes that another has authority over what we do and how we live—because identity in Christ recognizes that we are *not* our own. But in Christ, we never need to doubt our value, prove our worth, or compete for affirmation. God gives us all of these freely because God loves us like the world never can. We can know this truth, and this truth will set us free.

"I appeal to you therefore, brothers and sisters, on the basis of God's mercy, to present your bodies as a living sacrifice, holy and acceptable to God, which is your reasonable act of worship. Do not be conformed to this age, but be transformed by the renewing of the mind, so that you may discern what is the will of God—what is good and acceptable and perfect" (Romans 12:1–2). This invitation was written by the apostle Paul, who was a thoughtful, studious Jew who initially took the affirming pathway of human performance and strived to prove his worth (Philippians 3:4–6). Then he met Jesus and experienced the grace that got out in front of him on the road to Damascus (Acts 9). That's where God told him who he was. Listen to Paul's testimony in Philippians 3:4b–11 (MSG):

You know my pedigree: a legitimate birth, circumcised on the eighth day; an Israelite from the elite tribe of Benjamin; a strict and devout adherent to God's law; a fiery defender of the purity of my religion, even to the point of persecuting the church; a meticulous observer of everything set down in God's law Book. The very credentials these people are waving around as something special, I'm tearing up and throwing out with the trash—along with everything else I used to take credit for. And why? Because of Christ. Yes, all the things I once thought were so important are gone from my life. Compared to the high privilege of knowing Christ Jesus as my Master, firsthand, everything I once thought I had going for me is insignificant—dog dung. I've dumped it all in the trash so that I could embrace Christ and be embraced by him. I didn't want some petty, inferior brand of righteousness that comes from keeping a list of rules when I could get the robust kind that comes from trusting Christ—God's righteousness. I gave up all that inferior stuff so I could know Christ personally, experience his resurrection power, be a partner in his suffering, and go all the way with him to death itself. If there was any way to get in on the resurrection from the dead, I wanted to do it.

No wonder Paul makes a habit of introducing himself in his letters as a slave of Jesus Christ. He knows he is not his own—he belongs to Christ. He finds his meaning and belonging in Christ. He is loved and valued and affirmed by Christ. He is instructed and guided and taught by Christ. Paul belongs to Jesus. This is the same Paul who wrote, "I have been crucified with Christ, and it is no longer I who live, but it is Christ who lives in me. And the life I now live in the flesh I live by the faith of the Son of God, who loved me and gave himself for me" (Galatians 2:19b–20).

Prevenient grace is not merely a nice bit of theology that makes us feel good. Prevenient grace is where we begin to be human. It is how we begin to know who we are. It is the highway on-ramp to life. God has come to show us the way, and it all begins in knowing who we are by the prevenient grace of God.

JOURNALING AND REFLECTION

Pause to reflect on what you have read. What did you hear? Restate it in your own words. Make it your own. What is God pointing out in this chapter for you to think more about? What is God saying to you?

_____

_____

_____

_____

_____

_____

_____

_____

_____

_____

_____

_____

_____

_____

PRAYER

Tell God who you are. As you write this prayer to God, may the God who knit you together in your mother's womb, who knows every hair on your head and thought in your mind, who loves every inch of you—may this God be your identity, your way of life, and your meaning, through the power of his resurrected Son, Jesus.

DISCUSSION

1. Why has the belief that we belong to ourselves become a popular defense for doing as we please?

2. How does prevenient grace penetrate the lie that we are self-sovereign?

3. Why is it so easy to get caught up in the world's identity games?

4. Share about the moment when it dawned on you that you no longer belonged to yourself but found your identity in Christ.

5. How is Paul's testimony to the Philippians similar to or different from yours?

NOTES

NOTES

WEEK 4

I LIKES TO BE CHOSE

Talking about prevenient grace places us in the middle of an important conversation regarding divine election and predestination. There are two ways of thinking about this— Reformed or Wesleyan.

The Reformed (or, as some call it, Calvinist) understanding is that God has elected certain individuals to receive salvation. Another way of putting this is to say that God has "predestined" them to be saved, which would mean that God has also predetermined their response and their ability to accept God's gift of salvation. The Reformed perspective allows that the invitation to eternal security may be heard by all, but it maintains that only the elect are empowered to believe and be saved. Once a person is elected (chosen) by God, the grace of God is irresistible, which means they cannot overpower their election by resisting God's saving grace and making themselves "unsaved." Once they have been saved, there is nothing they can do to invalidate their salvation. They are eternally secure in Christ. This is a summary of the Reformed position, with acknowledgment that our Reformed friends may choose to explain it a little differently.

When Wesleyans speak of salvation, we say it is God's will that all be saved. Like the parables of the lost sheep, the lost coin, and the lost (or prodigal) son, Wesleyans affirm the belief that God goes out seeking every stray creature. God has predetermined, or predestined, that *all who believe in him* will be saved. In other words, Wesleyans believe that we all have a choice in the matter. Salvation

Our freedom to walk with Christ or turn away along the journey is sustained by God's gift of free will.

is offered to every human, but not every human responds to prevenient grace. God values our ability to choose and has given us the ability to accept *or* resist the gift of God's grace, rather than experiencing it as an irresistible force. What this means is that someone who accepts God's grace and is saved at one point in their life may choose, later in life, to reject that same grace, walk away from the path of God, and therefore lose the salvation they once had. Our freedom to walk with Christ or turn away along the journey is sustained by God's gift of free will.

Personally, I like the way the Wesleyans think because, in the words of Bob Benson, "I likes to be chose." Benson tells a story by that title in a book of collected Bob Benson stories called *"See You at the House."* In my younger days, Benson was a frequent preacher in the chapels at the university where I am currently president, and I can still close my eyes and see this thin, squeaky-voiced man standing before us and sharing what he was learning about God. In the story about being chosen, Benson shares his analogous understanding of God's prevenient grace as compared to Benson's personal experience as an undersize, non-athletic child. The QR code will take you to an audio recording on

It was not something in me
that made him call me.

YouTube of Benson telling the story himself, or a version of it can be read in excerpts below. I encourage you to listen if you can because Benson's voice is a gift to the story.

I was always a frail kid. I can remember when we used to go out to recess in grammar school. The two biggest and strongest kids in the class were always made captains of the softball teams. Usually they made themselves pitchers of the teams first, and then they picked the rest. One by one each kid was chosen—for athletic prowess, for friendship, for size—until everybody was on a team. Well, almost everybody.

"The game can't start until someone takes Bob," the teacher would insist.

And one of the captains would kick the dust and say in disgust, "We'll take him."

And I was usually sent to play behind the right fielder. I don't think I came up to bat until I was in the eighth grade. I wasn't too surprised to strike out then.

So, I likes to be *chose*.

. . .

So, I understand easily why it appears that I am both an implausible and illogical choice. I can only say that if it seems that way to those who only know a little about me, think how much more it is to me knowing all that I know about me. Fortunately my being chosen does not grow out of me, I am just a *choosee*.

The answer must be found in the heart of the *Chooser*. It was not something in me that made him call me. It was something in him. It began in his love for me.

And that is why these words of Jesus have such a lovely sound, "You did not choose me. I chose you."

It was not that I came upon Jesus Christ and, when I saw him, something within me ran out to meet him and, holding on to him, begged him to lift me out of myself and make me the person of my dreams. It was that he came upon me. His heart rushed out to me. He held on to me. He said he would make me the person that I wanted to be. He saw me. He loved me and chose me. I didn't find him. He found me.

. . .

But I wasn't chosen as a replacement for someone who didn't want to serve. I wasn't asked to play in the field someone was already covering. He saw me, he called me, he selected me, he picked me, he singled me out, he decided on me, he opted for me, he fixed upon me, he determined in favor of me, he preferred me, he espoused me. *He chose me.*

He did not refuse me, he did not reject me, he did not repudiate me, he did not spurn me, he did not dismiss me, he did not exclude me. He did not ignore, disregard, cast away, throw aside, or leave me out. *He chose me.*

It was not obligatory, mandatory, required, called for, deserved, necessary, imperative, compulsory, or forced. *He just chose me.*

It was his open, voluntary, willful, selective, deliberate, intentional choice. *He chose me.*

Out of his devotion, fondness, adoration, tenderness, affection, attachment, emotion, sympathy, empathy, and love, *he just chose me.*

And that has made all the difference in my life.[1]

---

1. Bob Benson, *"See You at the House": The Stories Bob Benson Used to Tell*, ed. R. Benson (Nashville: Generoux, 1986), 13, 14, 15.

JOURNALING AND REFLECTION

Pause to reflect on what you have read. What did you hear? Restate it in your own words. Make it your own. What is God pointing out in this chapter for you to think more about? What is God saying to you?

_____

_____

_____

_____

_____

_____

_____

_____

_____

_____

_____

_____

_____

_____

PRAYER

Thank God in your own words for the love that reached out to you when you were incapable of reaching out to God.

DISCUSSION

1. Some have said that, looking back over a long life, the Reformed version of salvation makes the most sense, that this is what God had in mind all along for them and that they were swept along by the grace they could not resist. Others have said that, looking into tomorrow, the Wesleyan version makes the most sense, that God has made us capable of responsible choice but has not forced anything on us. Which explanation makes the most sense to you?

2. Bob Benson says that being chosen is more about the heart of the chooser than the qualifications of the choosee. What does this mean?

3. Why are we prone to believe that we must make our-selves worthy of the grace of God? Where do we learn this?

4. How is the reality of God's loving, seeking, searching grace good news for the world today? How would you say this to someone who does not know God?

5. What have you learned and experienced about preve-nient grace over these last four weeks?

NOTES